*Good Babies, Bad Babies*

*Good Babies*
*Bad Babies*

JOHN LAWRENCE

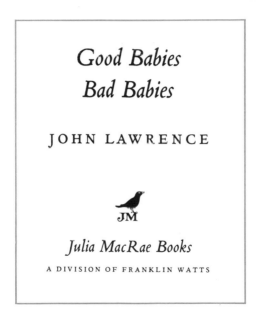

*Julia MacRae Books*

A DIVISION OF FRANKLIN WATTS

FOR TRISTAN

First published 1986 in a privately
printed black and white limited edition
This new edition first published 1987 by
Julia MacRae Books
A division of Franklin Watts
12a Golden Square
London, W1R 4BA
*and* Franklin Watts, Australia
14 Mars Road, Land Cove, NSW 2066
ISBN 0 86203 327 6
Printed in Singapore

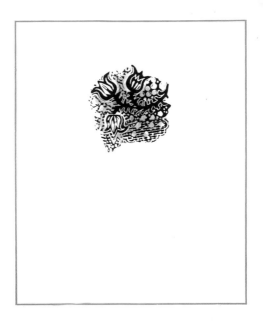

*Good Babies*

*Bad Babies*

*sweet ones, sour ones*

*bald ones, curly ones*

*big ones*

*small ones*

*and sometimes . . .*

*old fashioned ones*

*black ones*

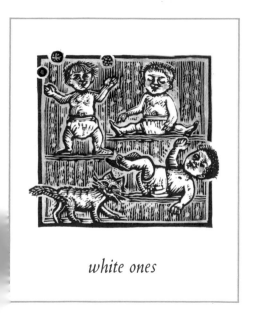

*white ones*

*fat ones*

*fin ones*

*and also very . . .*

*clever ones*

*loud ones*

*soft ones*

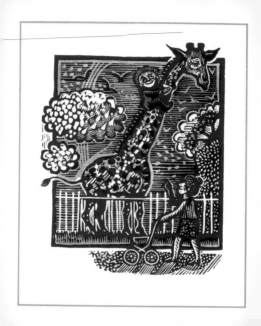

*high ones*

*low ones*

*and even . . .*

*dreams of glory ones*

*polite ones*

*rude ones*

*bouncing ones*

*tired ones*

*and lastly . . .*

*bye bye baby ones*

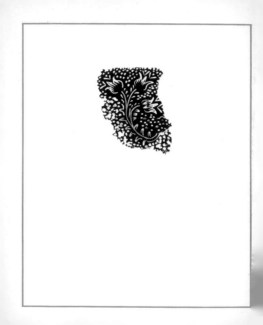